AROUND
DARLINGTON
IN OLD PHOTOGRAPHS

THE TEES AT LOW CONISCLIFFE, 1959, before Selset, Balderhead and Cow Green reservoirs were completed. The chimney, built in 1849, indicates Darlington waterworks Tees Cottage Pumping Station, where a beam engine of 1904 is still in steam from time to time.

AROUND
DARLINGTON
IN OLD PHOTOGRAPHS

COLLECTED BY
VERA CHAPMAN

ALAN SUTTON

Alan Sutton Publishing Limited
Phoenix Mill · Far Thrupp · Stroud · Gloucestershire

First published 1990

British Library Cataloguing in Publication Data

Chapman, Vera *1922–*
Around Darlington in old photographs.
1. Durham (County). Darlington, history
I. Title
942.836

ISBN 0–86299–812–3

Front Cover Illustration: WALWORTH CASTLE.

Typeset in 9/10 Korinna.
Typesetting and origination by
Alan Sutton Publishing Limited.
Printed in Great Britain by
Dotesios Printers Limited.

CONTENTS

To Ken, Gwen, Timothy, Andrew and Michelle.

PRIZEWINNER AT A LOCAL SHOW: Mrs Dorothy Arthur of Coatham Hall, Coatham Mundeville, as a girl c. 1930. (The *Northern Echo*).

INTRODUCTION

However well we know this countryside, old photographs bring home to us the changes in the physical and social environment since our great grandparents' days, and especially since the Second World War.

The horse, once dominant in travel, transport and farming, has all but disappeared except from sport and leisure. Farm labourers and craftsmen, and portable steam engines, have gone. The fields are empty of people most of the time, save for the lonely man (or woman) on a tractor, or the swift passage of a combine harvester. Traditional farm buildings cannot cope with large machines and massive crops, so are left to decay or are demolished in favour of huge sheds built of alien materials. The little ancillary buildings, lingering like ghosts from former ways of life, have been passing into oblivion – the gin-gangs and dovecotes, watermills and windmills, lime-kilns, toll-houses and smithies. Village schools, once thronged with children, have thinned and closed; village shops and pubs, post offices and ponds, one-man buses, village feasts and many unsophisticated pleasures have gone. Commuters and retired townspeople have moved in. Family mansions have become hotels and nursing homes.

On the other hand, hard labour and long hours in farm, quarry, shop and home have lessened. Rural roads are surfaced, piped water, sanitation, drainage, electricity and telephones have come to village and farm, and so has the car. The Tees, once productive of salmon and trout, then hit by pollution at its estuary, now shows signs of recovery. Notorious for its devastating floods, embanking, reservoir building and other measures have reduced this hazard on the river. The Skerne too, winding through Aycliffe and Barmpton, Great Burdon and Blackwell, which once powered twelve mills in as many miles and nourished eels, has been canalized and its floods controlled.

This is an essentially rural area of quality farmland ranging from heavy clays around Neasham and Burdon to the rolling uplands of Heighington and Aycliffe where the dolomite ridge swings over from Marsden Bay to cross the Tees at Piercebridge. The materials for vernacular building came from creamy dolomite to the north and west, brick to the south and east, cobbles near the Tees and a little red sandstone peeping through around Hurworth and Neasham, with clay pantiles initially imported from the Low Countries to replace the earlier thatch. This arable and pasture country, centred on Darlington market, was the locale of the audacious Shorthorn breeders who stocked the pastures of the New World. It was also the home of the world's first public railway, the Stockton and Darlington Railway, which spawned branches like a spider's web with Darlington at the centre, only to close in the 1960s and leave rural stations mainly in the memory.

This book of old photographs of the countryside around Darlington covers the former Darlington Rural District; from 1974 the extended Borough of Darlington, with the addition of Middridge and Aycliffe.

It is arranged as a tour, village by village, going west, north and east, and ending full circle along the river Tees. In each section you will move through one or more villages looking at scenes and buildings in the order of travel, and then meet the people. You may go, book in hand, and compare the scenes of today with those of yesterday, or simply do it in the mind's eye.

Low and High Coniscliffe

LOW CONISCLIFFE VILLAGE from Boat Lane, 1960. Perched on a gravel terrace above Tees flood levels, only a scatter of buildings bordered the former green until infilling and expansion began in the sixties.

THE TITHE BARN, 1960, which was then in a field on the north side of the village. Tithes were paid in produce to the parish church at High Coniscliffe. River cobble walls and pantiled roofs are typical of the old buildings in the two villages. The barn was later demolished.

THE UMBRELLA OAK, CONISCLIFFE MOOR, C. 1920. On a well-known ramblers' footpath, this old oak has since lost some lower branches and the pond is much smaller.

HIGH CONISCLIFFE MILL, 1964, converted to a house. An undershot wheel in the side building was powered by Ulnaby Beck. The beck was ponded back by a dam with a sluice gate and overhung with willows.

THE MILL, MILL POND AND VILLAGE FROM THE REAR, 1921. Photograph of a watercolour by an Australian visitor, M.F. Booth, bought by Elizabeth Thornton who lived in one of the tall houses on the right. The battlemented building nearby was a dovecote.

THE ENTRANCE TO HIGH CONISCLIFFE VILLAGE. By the eighteenth century land was quarried up for agricultural lime to the very walls of the churchyard, National School (now the village hall) and schoolmaster's house. The quarry is now overgrown and scarcely visible. An entrance drive on the left led to Coniscliffe Hall, the home of the Westolls, which was later destroyed by fire.

NOS 14–16 THE GREEN in 1907, with iron railings. The house on the right was High Coniscliffe Farm. All its farm buildings and two hinds' houses were demolished after the Second World War and built over.

A SCHOOL GROUP. St Edwin's Church tower and the schoolmaster's house are behind.

THE CHURCH INTERIOR, 1907, still lit by oil lamps. The screen was removed during Canon Wansey's incumbency.

CANON AND MRS WANSEY'S RETIREMENT PRESENTATION, 1974. Canon Wansey was previously for many years vicar of St Cuthbert's church, Darlington.

THE VICARAGE, 1907, at its greatest extent. A small eighteenth-century vicarage behind the church was later enlarged, then further extended in 1860 by the architect S.S. Teulon, who boldly jutted out bays over the steep quarry face. In 1967 the west kitchen wing and east end were demolished. It is now a private house on a dramatic site. Coniscliffe means 'king's cliff', and is named after the Saxon King Edwin of Northumbria and a natural riverbank rock outcrop.

THE VILLAGE, 1907. The row, newly built in 1895, contained the golf clubhouse and Mr Green the Pro's house (No. 20). Darlington Golf Club began here with nine holes by the Tees, and was enlarged behind the mill to eighteen holes by 1910. It moved to Haughton-le-Skerne in 1916.

A GOLF CLUB GROUP. Members at times wore loud blazers and panama hats, and came by horse and carriage, car, bicycle or train from town. The clubhouse had 'every comfort for the inner man'. Local lads acted as caddies at 1s. 6d. for two rounds, with an extra 6d. for cleaning the clubs. Children earned pennies by recovering golf balls.

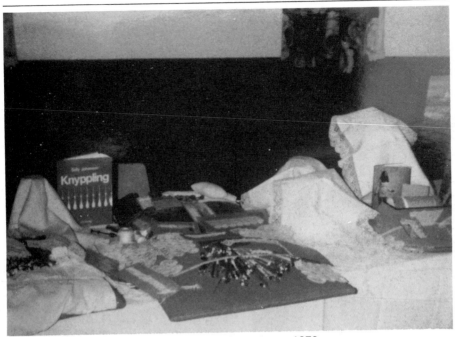

A PILLOW LACE DISPLAY at a High Coniscliffe WI meeting c. 1970.

THE OLD FOOTPATH FROM LOW TO HIGH CONISCLIFFE VIA ULNABY BECK, a right of way closed and diverted along by the Tees. J.B. (Bertie) Nicholson, photographed by his father C.P. Nicholson who died in 1944.

THE WEDDING in 1909 of Vera, daughter of James Westoll of Coniscliffe Hall, to James Scott Hindley. The wedding car was followed by the bridesmaids' horse-drawn carriage. Robert Lancaster is present in characteristic attire on the right (see page 33). James became the first Chairman of the National Coal Board on nationalization under the Atlee Government in 1946, and in 1948 was created Viscount Hyndley. He died in 1963.

THE LICENSEE AND FAMILY. Other pubs formerly included the Hare and Hounds, the Dog, the King of Sardinia and the Hark into Blue Cap. The Spotted Dog and the Duke of Wellington survive.

THE FISHERMEN'S CLUB based at the Duke of Wellington.

THE VILLAGE DRESSMAKER, Miss Shaw, lived at Cabin House on Dere Street, and retired to a cottage in High Coniscliffe on the south side, next to the then post office. As a young girl she helped to sew 'brushes' behind the hems of long dresses to protect them from mud.

AT ULNABY LANE CORNER WERE ROWS OF COBBLE BUILT COTTAGES and a shop, remembered as a general store and post office. This corner is now a car park for the Duke of Wellington. At the opposite corner was a small Wesleyan Chapel opened in 1827 and demolished after the last war.

THE DOVECOTE AT THE END OF A GARTH BEHIND THE GREEN, 1970, then being used as a saddle room, has since been converted into part of a dwelling named Tower House.

SECTION TWO

Carlbury and Piercebridge

CARLBURY CORNER. The Railway Inn and Bank House, c. 1910–20. On the left were the inn stables, next to which was a side door where Thomas R. Bell remembers sweets and lemonade being sold (ten toffees for a penny). Patrick Ratchford was a licensee, followed by the Misses Gardener. The inn, ruinous after the Second World War, was demolished when a by-pass replaced the old main road on the right. Dyance Beck drove Carlbury Mill near its confluence with the Tees.

THE WHEATSHEAF AND ENTRANCE TO PIERCEBRIDGE GREEN. The inn stables were to the right of the Wheatsheaf in the 1930s. The one-storey village shop and post office (centre) was where Michael Aislabie Denham (died 1859) collected local sayings and folklore, published by the Folk Lore Society in 1892 as *The Denham Tracts*.

THE TRIUMPH BUS served Coniscliffe, Piercebridge and Gainford. HN remained the Darlington registration until the 1970s. (Beamish)

LOCAL DEFENCE VOLUNTEERS, the Home Guard, outside the Railway Inn during the Second World War.

ZETLAND HUNT MEET ON PIERCEBRIDGE GREEN. The hunt used to hold its first and last meets of the season at Piercebridge, but changed to a Boxing Day meet.

THE NORTH-WEST CORNER OF PIERCEBRIDGE GREEN, 1966. Whitewashed houses and farmsteads denoted the properties of the Raby Estate. This was a carpenter's house and workshops, since sold off and then renovated as a private house. George Holmes was formerly a carpenter here.

THE VILLAGE SHOP AND POST OFFICE. Behind the counter are Basil Turner, Frances Turner and Maggie Thompson. In front are Norman Sims, Betty Race and Gordon Sims. Basil now runs the shop, and Gordon runs the Northern Nurseries near Carlbury Corner.

PIERCEBRIDGE SMITHY in the 1930s. Blacksmith Arthur Souter, father of Edna Richardson, came to the smithy before 1913 and died at the age of seventy-two, after which the smithy was closed, sold, and became a house, No. 11 The Green.

A PIERCEBRIDGE VILLAGE SCHOOL GROUP, 1929 or 1930. On the left is Mr Souter's daughter Edna (now Mrs Richardson). The boy on the left is Laurence Ratchford of the Railway Inn. Also pictured are Alfred, Hilda and Arthur Souter and the Hogg girls. The school had a bell cote. The date 1853 is over the porch. It closed in 1960, and is now the village hall.

CHILDREN IN FANCY DRESS ON THE GREEN for the village school's annual fête. Behind is the east side of the green.

CHILDREN 'DIGGING FOR VICTORY' IN THE SCHOOL GARDEN during the Second World War. The girl in the foreground may be Kathleen Brown of Bluebell cottages. One of the Bromfield boys is on the left. (The *Northern Echo*)

POLICEMAN'S COTTAGE, PIERCEBRIDGE. Photograph of a pastel drawing. Police Constable Reay came to this cottage c. 1890. His son was also a policeman in Darlington and Weardale and died in 1959 aged eighty-two. Theresa Reay, his granddaughter, inherited the drawing, but the cottage has disappeared. The police house within present memory has always been one on the east side of the green.

GRAVEL WORKING, 1963, near the Tees bank west of the village. On the cab of the crane is written John Graham Quarries Ltd. The Grahams lived at Barforth Hall, near Gainford. The gravel works were restored to farmland.

THE NORTH-EAST CORNER OF THE GREEN, in the early 1960s. Ivy House was still ivy-covered, and the green rough and damaged by parking. St Mary's church was rebuilt in 1873 with stone rescued from the restoration of Gainford church. The church gate is in memory of Richard George Holmes who died in 1948 aged one year and three months. The gate stoups are listed.

PIERCEBRIDGE ROMAN FORT, 1964. Kenneth, Timothy and Andrew Chapman look at an excavation trench in garths behind the east side of the village.

ARTHUR SOUTER, BLACKSMITH, C. 1930s, at the smithy door. The ring on the wall was for tying up horses.

ZETLAND HUNT RIDERS. Harry Walton, on the left, was a grain dealer from Gainford.

BILL CROOKS, THE HERDSMAN, CARRYING A BUNDLE OF STRAW. He was the cowman at Piercebridge Farm, and also a thatcher of rick roofs.

SHEEP SHEARING NEAR PIERCEBRIDGE, c. 1920. High Coniscliffe is in the distance. (Beamish)

THE GEORGE INN had a coach archway on the right, just off the photograph, and extensive stables. The road turns sharp right over the bridge which bore an inscribed stone, dated 1673. After the great Tees flood of 1771 it remained ruinous until repaired and widened on the downstream side in 1797. An archway of a chantry chapel of Our Lady, founded by the Baliols, remained at the other end of the bridge.

ROBERT LANCASTER, for thirty years licensee of The George Inn. 'The apparel marked the man.' A respected sporting character with a lifelong interest in horses, especially hackneys, he claimed to have attended every fair between John o' Groats and Land's End. Returning from America on the outbreak of the Civil War, he worked at the Turk's Head and the King's Head stables in Darlington and the Spotted Dog in High Coniscliffe. He retired from The George to Hackney Cottage in High Coniscliffe and died ten years later in 1917 aged eighty-five.

AT THE GEORGE INN, C. 1905. Jack Durham, father of Roly, and Mrs Elizabeth Durham, the nearer lady, are suggested identifications. The pony may be Bobby. Roly Durham ran the riding school and stables at The George, and Mr George Storrow can remember thirty-two horses there. The unmistakable Robert Lancaster is on the right.

THE HOUSE NEXT DOOR LATER BECAME PART OF THE GEORGE HOTEL by knocking through the adjoining wall in the present bar. A long case clock which finally stopped when the second of two Jenkins brothers licensees died is believed to have inspired the famous 'Grandfather's Clock' song. Menus here include Starters, Main Springs and Pendulum Puddings.

THE ZETLAND HUNT in a field near Piercebridge.

PIERCEBRIDGE STATION, C. 1940. Note the oil lamp, the signal box and the station master. Piercebridge was on the Stockton and Darlington Railway Company's Darlington and Barnard Castle line, opened in 1856, extended over the Pennines in 1861 and to Middleton-in-Teesdale in 1868. It became part of the North Eastern Railway in 1863, the LNER in 1923, and was closed in 1964.

THE STATION MASTER, MR COOPER, and his staff at the level crossing on Dere Street. At the station was a farmers' depot and a coal depot. Thomas Bell can recall that schoolchildren, c. 1935, bagged coal for a halfpenny a bag.

PULLING A TRAIN OF EMPTY WAGONS in January or February 1966 is engine No. 43056, an Ivatt 2–6–0 based in Darlington. After the line was closed for passengers, freight trains continued to use it for access to the branch line serving the Forcett Limestone Co.'s quarries across the Tees. (Photograph by T.J. Chapman)

THE SAME ENGINE, ex-LMS, heading a train of empty wagons to the Forcett quarries. Limestone was extensively used in the iron and steel industries of Teesside until their closure. (Photograph by T.J. Chapman)

BILLY GIBSON, farmer and milkman of Low Carlbury Farm, photographed in the mid-1940s on Dere Street near the station.

FRED DENT, FARMER, OF HIGH CARL-BURY FARM, also taken in the 1940s, on Piercebridge station platform in snow.

Walworth, Summerhouse, Houghton-le-Side, Killerby and Coatsay Moor

WALWORTH CASTLE GATE LODGE, designed in 1877 by G.G. Hoskins FRIBA of Darlington and built by Adamsons of Gainford for Gerald P.V. Aylmer. Dun House and Houghton Bank stone were used, with hearths made of Stainton stone.

THE NORTH-EAST CORNER OF WALWORTH CASTLE C. 1920. The parapet urns were taken down, a lake filled in and the gardens opened out when the castle became a residential school after the Second World War. It is now a hotel.

THORNTON HALL, STAINDROP ROAD, C. 1960, on a frosty morning. The front is an early sixteenth-century manor house built by the Tailboys of Hurworth, with some original windows, carved beams and a plaster ceiling. Its rear extension by the Bowes or the Salvins in the seventeenth century has a fine Jacobean staircase. It has long been a farmhouse.

THE SOUTH FRONT OF WALWORTH CASTLE WAS BUILT BY THOMAS JENISON in the late sixteenth century, probably on the remnants of a medieval fortified house of the Hansard family. The west wing was rebuilt in 1864 by John H. Aylmer who died four years later with his wife and eldest son in the Abergele railway disaster. The occasion of the photograph is unknown.

WALWORTH GATE SMITHY. Mr Wanless was the blacksmith. Nearby was a toll-house.

WALWORTH GATE TOLL-HOUSE. The 'gate' was the toll-bar or turnpike serving the Sunderland Bridge to Piercebridge Turnpike Road of 1748, which passed by Walworth Castle.

THROSTLE NEST FARMHOUSE, Walworth Gate, in 1903, demolished in 1939 in the time of Albert W. Hewitson. In the photograph are William Hewitson's children: at the gate, Henry Scorer Hewitson, who later farmed at Castle Farm, Walworth; by the door Mary, Edith and Helena. Edith is (Dec. 1989) at Cold Comfort Farm, Neasham, aged ninety-nine.

HOUGHTON-LE-SIDE, 1960. Farm with a circular, stone dovecote incorporated in the buildings. Whitewashed farmsteads are part of the Raby Estate.

BOLAM QUARRY. A basalt dyke begins in the Hebrides and crosses Cockfield Fell to the Cleveland Hills and Robin Hood's Bay. It was quarried at Houghton-le-Side and Bolam in the eighteenth century for turnpike road stone, and later also for surface chippings. Bolam Quarry, where the dyke was broader, was finally worked out in 1965 in building the Darlington by-pass.

THE RABY HUNT INN, SUMMERHOUSE, and the Bowron children, c. 1900. Their father, William Bowron, was a joiner and undertaker, and licensee of the Raby Hunt. Fred holds the donkey, Minnie, Clarie and Bella (?) are ready for a ride. Their grandfather was also a joiner, undertaker and licensee, and made furniture which was sold by subscription. His joiner's shop was on the green in front of the pub.

GEORGE BOWRON, SANITARY ENGINEER, AND HIS GANG. George, the eldest child of William Bowron, licensee of the Raby Hunt Inn, died at the age of twenty-seven in the 'flu epidemic of 1919.

LAURIE GRAHAM WAS RELATED TO THE BOWRONS OF SUMMERHOUSE. He was the High Coniscliffe postmaster during the First World War, aided by Minnie Bowron who carried letters to Walworth Castle, where the butler ironed them before handing them to the Palmers who rented the castle. Laurie played the violin at pubs, etc. for local dances.

KILLERBY, 1968. A derelict farmstead on the south side of the former village green, demolished soon after this time. Linear buildings were typical until the eighteenth century, when improvements in stock breeding and new fodder crops introduced foldyards for cattle fattening.

THE BOWRON FAMILY C. 1900, in the garth where cars now park for the Raby Hunt. In the photograph are William, licensee, his wife Louisa (one of Robert Lancaster's daughters of The George, Piercebridge) and children George, on the right, Clarie, Minnie and Bella, and Fred on horseback. Their donkey is on the right, and a tent on the left.

COATSAY MOOR FARM, near Heighington, 1965. A doorway with Queen Anne's head, crown and the date 1713. Queen Anne died in 1714; of her seventeen children, only one, William, Duke of Gloucester, survived infancy, and he died at the age of ten.

COATSAY MOOR FARM DOVECOTE AND POND, 1965. An entrance 'lantern' at the apex has since been added. Brick quoins brace creamy dolomite walls. Doves or pigeons provided fresh meat, eggs and strong manure.

COATSAY MOOR FARM GIN-GANG AND POND, 1965. The horse wheel, gin-gang or jenny-ring was the first machine applied to farming. From the 1790s, yoked horses worked a thresher and chopper in the barn by a system of gear wheels.

Heighington and Redworth

WEST GREEN, HEIGHINGTON, C. 1960. The Bay Horse is on the right. Other West Row properties are still much the same today. Some now have porches and have changed their windows. The green was gated, and served as a bleaching ground for Heighington linen weavers.

THE VILLAGE POND AND PARISH CHURCH. The pond was at the low end of West Green. It was fed by surplus water from the nearby 'Pant', the stone building on the green which housed a public pump supplied from an underground storage cistern. The pond used to be crowded with geese on their way to Darlington market or local farms. A goat sits near the church gate.

THE WATER BARREL was presumably for distributing water drawn from the pant and its reservoir.

THE NORTHERLY EXIT FROM THE GREEN TO SHILDON was narrow until the shop and row of buildings on the right was demolished in 1926. The newly widened road was opened in 1927.

THE SHOP WHICH WAS DEMOLISHED WAS BROWNLESS' GROCERY AND POST OFFICE. John Brownless was an auctioneer and valuer. Advertised on the windows were Lingford's baking powder, made by the Lingfords at Bishop Auckland, and Rowntree's cocoa and chocolate made at York; both were Quaker family firms with model factories. The Lingford label had a picture of a heather moor, ling being the northern name for heather.

CHILDREN outside a house on Darlington Road, facing West Green.

HEIGHINGTON CORN MILL ON MILL BANK, since demolished.

SHOP ON CHURCH VIEW.

ST MICHAEL'S PARISH CHURCH, before removal of the creepers. The church built by the Hansards of Walworth on Saxon foundations is contemporary with Durham Cathedral and retains its Norman tower, chancel arch and belfry openings. It has a pre-Reformation pulpit, c. 1500, possibly the oldest in the country. Three bells of c. 1400 are named Peter, Paul and Mary, and three of 1882 are named Faith, Hope and Charity.

THE BLACKSMITH'S SHOP near Trafalgar House on the old road to Aycliffe. One of the men is Batty Wright. Beech Crescent now occupies the site.

A THRESHING MACHINE being pulled out of Manor Farm yard on East Green.

RIDGE AND FURROW, 1967, near Trafalgar House, a now increasingly rare survival, destroyed here in making the village by-pass. Broad ridge and furrow, about seven yards wide, with a reversed S curve, was originally formed by long, eight-oxen plough teams in the Middle Ages. Most has disappeared, deliberately 'thrown down' or 'ploughed out', especially since tractors became widespread.

HEIGHINGTON SHOW SHEEP LINE-UP. The show was first held in 1876.

THE 150TH ANNIVERSARY CAVALCADE nearing Heighington station from Shildon. *Locomotion No. 1* drew the train on 27 September 1825, the opening day of the world's first steam-hauled public railway, the Stockton and Darlington Railway. The original is in Darlington Railway Museum. A replica was specially made in the region for these celebrations, with Mike Satow in charge. Following is a chaldron wagon, c. 1870, of 53 hundredweight capacity, a type marked L, which carried Lord Londonderry's coal from pit to ship at Seaham Harbour. A chaldron wagon is now the symbol of Beamish Open Air Museum.

THE FLYING SCOTSMAN followed by 910 NER, an engine also now in Darlington Railway Museum.

THE LEVEL CROSSING, HEIGHINGTON STATION. On the right is the original S & DR platform, with a low, cobbled surface and the early station building. On the left the large platform was built to serve the wartime munitions factory which became the site for the Aycliffe Industrial Estate, bringing in its wake the new town of Newton Aycliffe.

REDWORTH HALL, 1968, a rear view in snow. The seventeenth-century house, formerly the home of the Surtees family, was much enlarged over the years. It became a residential school, and is now a hotel and conference centre. The wall separates the park from Redworth village green.

OLD FARMHOUSE ON EAST GREEN, Heighington. It had been the manor house, built c. 1620, and bears a scroll pediment over the doorway.

Middridge and Aycliffe

VIEW OVER MIDDRIDGE VILLAGE GREEN from the east end. North Row, on the right, included the King's Arms, Colliery Farm, several cottages, a school and master's house and, on the right, the Mason's Arms. The gardens on the left were one acre of the green enclosed by agreement in 1864 by Sir William Eden of Windlestone Hall.

CUMBANK HOUSE, built in 1901 by the Dennis family. Annie Miller Dennis was the postmistress here for twenty years. Her family history shows a connection with Prof. Hugh Miller, the eminent Scottish geologist, writer and theologian. On the right are two of the five cottages later demolished, the space forming the entrance to the Bay Horse car park.

MIDDRIDGE, C. 1924. Children standing in line before marching into school. The school was to the right. All the buildings opposite, including the Mason's Arms, have been demolished.

NORTH ROW in the 1920s. The pit-head winding gear of Middridge Colliery is just visible. This northern end of the row included Hall Farm and cottage and a single-storey butcher's shop built forward on to the green.

THE SHILDON ROAD LEAVING MIDDRIDGE in the 1920s passed under the bridge of the mineral railway which linked Middridge Colliery to the Darlington and Bishop Auckland line.

A SCHOOL GROUP OUTSIDE THE MIDDRIDGE CHURCH OF ENGLAND SCHOOL, C. 1875. Five members of the Dennis family are in the photograph.

CHILDREN FILING PAST THE FRONT OF THE SCHOOL. The building had a chancel at one end, and was used for Sunday services. It is now the village hall.

J. NEASHAM'S DRAPER'S SHOP, was in the south-west corner of the green, beyond the Bay Horse. The Dodds, who had previously been butchers, and then farmed at Colliery Farm, next ran the shop. It is now Mr Mellor's.

A SCHOOL GROUP, C. 1924, with their teacher, Miss Mann. The children include three Dodds, one or two Birches, one Spowart, Willie Johnson and Foster Davies.

MOTOR COACH OUTSIDE THE BAY HORSE. Behind the inn sign on the green was a central block with a shop and post office, since demolished.

AYCLIFFE HIGH STREET in 1907. This was the Great North Road between London and Edinburgh! The horseman may be John Brown of East Ketton Farm, or George Chapman, owner of West Quarry (limestone), who lived at the large house on the left.

AYCLIFFE HIGH STREET. The vicarage gateway was overhung by trees. Seated are Mr Robinson and Mr Parker. All the right-hand houses and the vicarage have gone. The distant house was demolished when a by-pass was built.

THE RAM INN AND THE ROYAL TELEGRAPH are still on the part of the Great North Road now by-passed. The Ram's licensee was also a butcher. Mr Stivison lived at the house on the right.

JUBILEE SCHOOL, AYCLIFFE, replaced the old National School on the green in 1897 for Queen Victoria's Diamond Jubilee. George Scott's grandfather built it. It is now the village hall, with new school buildings behind it.

THE NATIONAL SCHOOL was enlarged in 1833 and in 1882, and could accommodate 250 children. Its site, towards the south side of the green, is now quite open.

THE SKERNE AT AYCLIFFE. The Old Mill House on the right is now the home of George Scott, a builder, who built for the Eldon Estates. Maddrick's miller's horse and cart was going towards the green.

THE COUNTY HOTEL, facing Aycliffe green. The rest of North Row has been demolished.

AYCLIFFE VILLAGE GREEN and a 'pump of pure water'. The road led down to the mill and the Skerne. On the left are the houses on North Row which have now gone.

AYCLIFFE WINDMILL TOWER, in 1965. Built of local dolomite, the cap, here missing, would turn, taking the sails into the eye of the wind. Most Durham windmills were out of action by the end of last century. The iron ladder indicates its use as an ARP watch tower during the Second World War. The Durham motorway now passes below it. In the distance is Aycliffe parish church.

A SAXON CROSS SHAFT stood in St Andrew's churchyard on its original base. Sculpted with interlace patterns and animals of late tenth-century date, it has been removed for safe keeping.

THE SHRUBBERY, AYCLIFFE.

AYCLIFFE WEST QUARRY was owned by George Chapman. The Noble brothers are in this photograph. The dolomite, or magnesian limestone, was used for agricultural lime, as a flux in the iron and steel industry of Teesside, and latterly for insulating materials.

Coatham Mundeville, Brafferton, Ketton, Beaumont Hill and Whessoe

PLOUGHING COMPETITION in a field called the High Garth at Coatham Mundeville opposite the Foresters' Arms. On the left is Coatham Hall before the wall and part of the grounds were removed to widen the A1. On the right, Glebe House was farmed by Bill Lawson's grandfather, seen in a bowler hat to the right. The central figure, also in a bowler, is probably Mr Ellwood, grandfather of Mrs Nixon, who farmed at Brafferton. The plough holder wears two medals.

GLEBE HOUSE, Coatham Mundeville, also called Hallgarth Farmhouse, although there are no farm buildings adjacent. Bill Lawson now farms from here. Venetian windows, Gothic tracery and semicircular front gardens were fashionable in the Georgian period. The iron railings have now gone.

THE LONELY CHURCH OF ST MARY MAGDALENE, Coatham Mundeville, in the 1920s. A chapel of ease to Haughton-le-Skerne parish church, it was built in 1865 to the design of R.J. Withers, and seated 130. In 1929 it was taken into Aycliffe parish, but is now a house and remains unchanged externally.

WHILEY HILL LEVEL CROSSING, in the 1920s, on the original Stockton and Darlington Railway line.

WHILEY HILL COTTAGE, 1931. Built in 1825 for the opening of the Stockton and Darlington Railway, it still bears the company's plaque, S & DR 1. Listed for historical reasons, it is possibly the first railway cottage ever built.

DRESSING UP AT HALLGARTH HOUSE, Coatham Mundeville, the home of Mr and Mrs Thomas Summerson, photographed here in the garden. The seventeenth- and eighteenth-century house is now a hotel.

COATHAM MUNDEVILLE MILL AND WEIR, 1930. A corn mill on the Skerne was converted into a four-storey linen-shoe thread mill by Thomas Porthouse, co-inventor and patentee in 1787, with John Kendrew of Darlington, of the first flax-spinning machinery. The mill employed sixty. About 1860, however, it was dismantled to revert to corn milling. Counter gearing and an 8 x 18 ft undershot wheel were installed in 1884 after a fire. Barley meal was still being ground in the 1960s. Once a post office, it now serves as dwellings.

BRAFFERTON CORN MILL, c. 1909. Photograph of a painting done by Mr K. Firby of Manor Farm when a boy. Much of the stone was used to build a new village hall on the green, leaving only one ruined building. The Skerne powered ten mills in quick succession in and north of Darlington.

BRAFFERTON VILLAGE, with the former village hall on the green. Brafferton means 'village on the broad ford'.

BRAFFERTON WI commemorated their golden jubilee in 1965 by planting a pink hawthorn tree on the village green. Left to right: Mesdames Bellerby, Smith (Irene, local historian), Raine, Duff, Burton, Robinson, Farrow and Brown.

MARE AND FOAL AT BRAFFERTON. Ambrose Binks Firby, grandfather of Mrs B.E. Futter, touches the foal near a field barn where bungalows now stand. The lad is probably Billy Smith.

BRAFFERTON SCHOOL GROUP, c. 1955. An oval date plaque between the school windows reads 1823. The teacher's house is on the left. Hubert Ord later became the head of Staindrop school. In the centre, Jean Elstob; on the right, Kathleen Fuller, Margaret Snowball and Judith Spears; on the front row, in light dress, Janet Robinson and, end left, Sheila Wilkinson; back left, John Hall. The school closed in 1960.

KETTON HALL before tripartite windows were inserted, the portico lowered and foliage removed. The hall was the home of Charles Colling, renowned pioneer breeder of Shorthorn cattle, at whose retirement sale in 1910 'Comet' was sold, the first bull ever to fetch 1,000 guineas. The Colling beech is said to have been planted in the sale enclosure.

KETTON BRIDGE, 1934. This packhorse bridge was reached by a causeway raised on brick arches to avoid floods. Its dolomite parapets are splayed at both ends, and the surface is cobbled. The bridge was left high and dry after the Skerne's meanders were canalized.

A STACKYARD AT KETTON, pre-1914, on one of the Brown family's farms. In the 1890s they farmed East Ketton, Little Ketton and Lovesome Hill. The ladder and loose straw suggests that the haystacks were being thatched.

LOW BEAUMONT HILL FARMHOUSE, pre-1930. Mrs Reed (née Bramwell) and her son Maurice on a visit to the Browns who farmed there then. Her daughter, Roma, recalls oil lamps and candles up to 1930, when her visits ceased. There was no indoor sanitation, a 'three-holer' down the garden was used. However, you could pick fruit from the bedroom window.

AN LNER MAIN LINE TRAIN, pre-1930, approaches Low Beaumont Hill underpass, headed by an 'Atlantic' class 4–4–2. The Newcastle and Darlington Junction Railway of 1844 became in 1846 the York, Newcastle and Berwick and, in 1847, the North Eastern Railway. After re-grouping in 1923 it was the LNER and upon nationalization in 1948 it became British Rail.

METHODIST WOMEN'S OUTING TO LOW BEAUMONT HILL FARM to the Misses Brown, who appear at either end of the back row. The Brown family left the farm in 1930.

WHESSOE GRANGE BARN, 1961. This sixteenth-century manor house remained until a few years ago, a survivor of the otherwise lost village of Whessoe. Long used as a farm building with a gin-gang attached, stone-mullioned windows and two arched window heads in the left-hand gable end betrayed its origin.

A TUDOR FIREPLACE IN WHESSOE GRANGE BARN. Traditionally the barn was called a chapel, the only evidence being some buried human bones. Possibly it was the parlour and solar wing of a once larger house. Two areas of wall paintings survived. It was demolished in the 1980s.

Bishopton and Great Stainton

THE CROSS AND GREEN, BISHOPTON, beside St Peter's church. The base and shaft of the old cross were moved into the churchyard in 1883, when the present cross, a gift of the vicar, the Revd Charles H. Ford, was erected. The green is now railed.

ST PETER'S CHURCH INTERIOR, still lit by oil lamps. The church was rebuilt in 1846. Its outer walls incorporate medieval grave fragments and a sundial of 1776. The gothic reredos of Caen stone is to the memory of Mr Ford, vicar for thirty years. The Parish Feast was held on St Peter's day.

BISHOPTON VICARAGE.

THE VICAR.

THE VICAR'S HANDYMAN, who was also his driver and groom, and cared for the vicarage grounds.

BISHOPTON SCHOOL, GROUP III, c. 1890s. The schoolmaster on the left, Samuel Mills, was also the treasurer of the village football team.

GREAT STAINTON SCHOOL GROUP, 1963, on the closure of the school. Photographed here in the school yard are all the children at that date, with their teacher Mrs F.A. Hill. She and the children transferred to Bishopton school.

TEACHERS AT BISHOPTON SCHOOL, c. 1890s. The seated teacher looks like Samuel Mills again.

BISHOPTON HOPPINGS, OR SHOW DAY, an occasion for wearing one's best clothes. On the far right is Horace Hill.

AN OPEN AIR SERVICE. The occasion may be the Hoppings, Show Day, Sports Day, or the Parish Feast held in June near to St Peter's day. Mrs Scott recalls that farmers gave tea on the green. In the evening there were races for children in a garth behind Grange Farm and a dance.

BISHOPTON HOPPINGS. A brass band and procession assembles by the bridge over Bishopton Beck.

MAYPOLE DANCING on the village green, prior to 1943.

BISHOPTON FOOTBALL TEAM, 1897/8. S. Mills (treasurer), the Revd H.J. Watford (president). Back row, left to right: J. Thompson, A. Thompson, Hutton Trotter, W. Carter (goal), C. Orwin (captain), H. Mills (secretary). Front row: T. Duff, F. Morris, S. Parish, E. Moore, Harry Trotter, E. Nicholson (trainer).

A BISHOPTON PAIR. Is it Reggie Callender and his sister? Or a policeman?

TWO CALLENDER CHILDREN, aged three and two and a half, a studio photograph given 'to Aunt Lena, 1899'. Probably Reggie and Minnie. Aunt Lena died in 1979.

REGGIE AND MINNIE CALLENDER, aged seven and five, another photograph given 'to Aunt Lena'. Reggie was killed on 5 October 1915, by accidentally pulling a pin out of a hand grenade during a demonstration and throwing himself on to it to save others. He was in 17 'B' attached 9th Durham Light Infantry and was buried in France.

RAYMOND HILL, c. 1940, holding the rein of Bishopton butcher Henry Callender's cart horse.

W.H.P. HILL (HORACE) OF BISHOPTON as a young man. Born in 1899, he died in 1989, aged almost ninety.

READY FOR HARVEST FESTIVAL, BISHOPTON. A model corn rick prepared by a thatcher, probably a man from Stainton. Bent hazel twigs peg down the thatched roof. Note the hand shears for trimming.

LEASES HOUSE, No. 1 Church View, Bishopton, a brick and pantiled house typical of the area. It stands between the Talbot Inn and Town Farm. Mr and Mrs C. Callender are at the gate. Lease or leaze means pasture or meadow.

THE BISHOPTON BUTCHER, HENRY CALLENDER. Mrs Scott remembers him as wearing a brown trilby hat, greasy on top.

Sadberge, Great Burdon and Barmpton

SADBERGE GREEN, c. 1930s. The Jubilee Stone, a larger boulder found in excavations for Sadberge reservoir, was set up in 1887 for Queen Victoria's Golden Jubilee. It recalls Sadberge as a once separate county and Victoria as Countess of Sadberge. Burnet's Row, behind the seat, was replaced c. 1937–8 by Hillside Terrace.

TOWN FARM AND SADBERGE GREEN in the 1930s. A donkey and goat graze the green. The farmhouse is now Tithe House and its outbuildings to the left have been demolished. Cricket was allowed on the green near Town Farm provided that play stopped when a vehicle passed by. Sadberge Feast, with roundabouts, donkey rides and coconut shies, was held on the green.

SADBERGE CRICKET TEAM, pre-1913. The umpire was John Adamson. On the right was Joseph Shepherd of Prospect House, a retired farmer, who died in August 1913. Back row: third from left, John E. Shepherd; fourth, Matt Hall, village joiner, and fifth, Ernest T. Shepherd, farmer. Front right, lying on the grass, G.W. Goldsborough.

CHAPEL ROW, SADBERGE. Raby House, with the railings, was the home from the early 1800s of the owners of a tan-yard at the rear, down the hill.

THE TAN-YARD WORKERS, 1925–6. Kneeling, front: J.R. Holland; from the left: Jack Parnaby, Fred Lightfoot, Abner Binks, Jack Binks, Keith Holland, Bill Pybus and his father J. Pybus. When sold in 1891, the tannery had seventy-four pits, steam-heated drying sheds, bark barns and leather warehouses, and it produced eighty hides per week. It was burned down c. 1943, but by that time was used only for storage.

SADBERGE NATIONAL SCHOOL GROUP, 1891. John Bolton, schoolmaster. Next to him, Ernest Shepherd, aged eight. The school log book for 1891 reported: 'The children had their photographs taken last Monday by Mr Tiley of Middlesbrough' and that many children in the upper standard were absent on 2 November, potato picking. The building, dating from 1870, is now the village hall.

A PLANE TREE was planted on Sadberge green on 6 May 1935 by Christopher Shepherd, centre, aged eighty-seven, the oldest resident, to celebrate the Silver Jubilee of George V. The Revd Peter Belshaw presided, Frank Crowson is slightly behind, and Harold Shepherd is moving forward. Sports for the children were held in Beacon Hill Field, and there was tea and a dance at the Memorial Institute in the evening. This was a wooden hut brought from Ripon Camp and opened in 1921 with a Roll of Honour to sixty men who served in the First World War. Its site is now occupied by three bungalows.

THE BUCK INN, SADBERGE. Walter Willson, a well-known local grocery firm, had a business in Northgate, Darlington, in the 1890s. Stables and smithies were important adjuncts in country and town until the Second World War.

STOOKING SHEAVES OF OATS at West Newbiggin, 1966. Reapers and binders and the stooking of corn disappeared rapidly in the 1960s as combine harvesters took over.

A STOOKED FIELD, 1966, between Newbiggin and The Mitre, one of the last areas around Darlington to retain traditional harvesting.

THE BAR AT THE THREE TUNS, Sadberge, with the old pumps and decor. Left to right: Eddie Wallace of an old village family, Lillie Armitage, Clifford Cockburn, Betty Walters and Jean Wallace. Betty has now been licensee here for thirty-seven years.

THE THREE TUNS, C. 1960. From the left: Norman Wilkinson, Betty Walters, her sister Lillie Armitage, Charlie Harrison (butcher) and Norman Wilkinson's son Norman.

GREAT BURDON C. 1920. The Black Horse pub was demolished for widening this road which now leads into a dual carriageway to Stockton.

A FLOOD AT GREAT BURDON OLD BRIDGE. The Skerne's meanders have been straightened and embanked to prevent floods. Burdon bridge was replaced after the First World War by one with an iron parapet.

A HEXAGONAL GIN-GANG OR JENNY-RING, 1964, behind a small barn on the east side of Great Burdon green. Gin and jenny were shorter names for the engine worked by horses yoked to turn an overhead wheel. This meshed with gears which worked threshing and chopping machinery in the barn. Steam threshing made horse wheels redundant.

GREAT BURDON SMITHY, beside the green, continued to work until recently.

BARMPTON GRAVEL QUARRY, in 1979, was excavating late Ice Age gravels for roadstone. Disturbed ground on the right was typically colonized by wild poppies.

BARMPTON HALL was the home of Robert Colling, like his brother Charles of Ketton Hall, a noted Shorthorn breeder.

Middleton St George and Middleton One Row

FIGHTING COCKS STATION, on the original line of the Stockton and Darlington Railway, was by-passed when Bank Top station was built and the line re-routed via Geneva Junction. The photograph may record preparations for the centenary celebrations in 1925.

THE KILLINGHALL ARMS, MIDDLETON ST GEORGE in The Square stands opposite The Havelock Arms. Both names recall prominent landowning families in Middleton.

DEMOLITION DAY on a Sunday morning after the Second World War. A blast furnace chimney was brought down by the method now familiarized in Fred Dibner's recent TV programmes, by burning timber on one side of the base until it collapsed in that direction. The remnants were then blasted.

THE SQUARE, MIDDLETON ST GEORGE. A drinking trough for horses surrounds the central gas lamp. A gasworks began in Middleton in 1871 and in the 1890s Middleton had thirty-two public lamps. A police station stands on the site of the far terrace.

OFFICERS' MESS, BOMBER STATION, MIDDLETON ST GEORGE, spring 1945. Aircrews of the Royal Canadian Air Force lounge in front. Whitley, Halifax, Wellington and Lancaster bombers operated from what became in 1964 a civil airport. The mess is now the St George Hotel. The Sergeants' Mess, Station HQ, guard room, central tower, hangars and cinema are all still there, mainly serving other uses.

THE LOST VILLAGE OF WEST HARTBURN, deserted in the sixteenth century. A peasant farmstead was excavated in 1964 by Teesside Archaeological Society. The former village green lies to the right, with Foster House Farm in the distance. In the two photographs are Dr Brian Dobson, archaeologist and director, Leslie Still, Alan Pallister and Joan Southeran.

LOW MIDDLETON HALL, C. 1970, where Miss Hester Duff then lived, in recent years the home of the Turton family. The handsome façade raised in the eighteenth century by the Killinghalls disguises a much older house. Pauline Haslam is now developing a small centre for education in the cultural and creative use of leisure here.

THE DOVECOTE, LOW MIDDLETON HALL, in 1920. The brick, octagonal cote on a stone plinth still had its entrance lantern on top. Inside were 1,500–2,000 nesting holes. The doorway was later blocked.

THE OLD PARISH CHURCH OF ST GEORGE, C. 1950. It fell into disrepair after St Laurence's was built nearer to the growing residential village in 1871. The tower was added in 1883, but later began to lean away and was demolished C. 1960 after being declared unsafe.

A FOOTPATH BY THE TEES NEAR MIDDLETON ONE ROW, C. 1913. The spire of St Laurence's can be seen in the distance. (Beamish).

A MEET AT THE DEVONPORT HOTEL, Middleton One Row. The hotel had been rebuilt with much of the village c. 1820 when Dinsdale Spa was flourishing, and has now been considerably refurbished.

MIDDLETON ONE ROW, c. 1890. Its twelve-acre green includes the steep bank of the Tees, threaded with paths made for visitors to the spa. (Beamish)

THE RIVERSIDE PATH, C. 1813, leading upstream to the spa well and baths. Middleton One Row can be seen through the trees, perched high above a bend in the Tees. (Beamish)

SCENE AT DINSDALE SPA. Photograph of an 1833 print. Smoke rises from the spa baths beside the Tees. Above stands the seventy-bedroom hotel of 1829, designed by Ignatius Bonomi for Lord Durham, who also developed the woodland walks. As the spa declined, it became a hotel for mental invalids and later a residential school for handicapped children.

Dinsdale and Sockburn

DINSDALE STATION TOOK A PRIDE IN ITS GARDENING. The ticket office was on the road bridge above, from which the photograph was taken. Note the clerestory coaches. The long terrace in the background was built to house Dinsdale Iron Works families.

DINSDALE SPA GOLF CLUB. THE NEWCASTLE CUP COMPETITION, intercounty foursomes, 1922. The winners were A.H. Grieveson and D.A. Haggie.

DINSDALE SPA GOLF CLUB. EXHIBITION MATCH, 1958. J.C. Gibb, captain; Bobby Locke and David Mc Moffat; Eric Lester and Derek Munro. Bobby Locke, a well-known golfer, was third from the left.

CAPTAIN'S DAY GROUP, 1935, outside the old club house, formerly the Spa Baths and Hotel. Left to right, back row: J.J. Peck (secretary), E. Pybus (greenkeeper), -?-, -?-, W. Gordon, A. Webster, W. Andrews. Middle row, seated: J. Hedley, E. Mann, W. Dunne, S.N. McQuistan, G. Pugh, H. Humphries. On grass: E. Williamson, -?-, K. Hounam.

EXHIBITION MATCH, 31 August 1958, at Dinsdale Spa Golf Club. Bobby Locke drives.

CUTTING OATS WITH A MANUAL REAPER near Dinsdale, c. 1900. One man has a wooden rake, three are holding bands and one is tying a sheaf. The sheaves stand upright, but are not yet stooked. The old Spa Hotel and the bath house are in the distance. (Beamish)

DIPPING SHEEP NEAR DINSDALE BRIDGE. A rector of Dinsdale in 1839 built a wooden bridge on stone piers over the Tees to link his two estates. A later, arched bridge collapsed, killing two workmen. This light iron bridge was built by J. Emerson. The old toll cottage and bell still stand at the bridge end. (Beamish)

OVER DINSDALE HALL, built in 1903 by MacKenzie of Darlington for R. Thompson, Esq., to a design of Hugh Hedley.

PLOUGHING STUBBLE AT LOW DINSDALE, C. 1900. William Megson is using an iron-wheeled plough pulled by two horses. (Beamish)

MOWING ABOVE BATH COTTAGES, Dinsdale, C. 1900. One man is forking the grass. A child also holds a fork. (Beamish)

GOING TO SCHOOL AT LOW DINSDALE, c. 1913. On the right are the rectory and the church of St John the Baptist, the tower of which was built in 1196. Sculptured fragments of an earlier church are built into the porch. (Beamish)

LOW DINSDALE SCHOOL, c. 1900. The children are going home carrying their own books and slates. The tiny school was built in 1851 on land given by Mr Surtees of Dinsdale Manor. The school is now a house. (Beamish)

THE KEEPER'S COTTAGE, Dinsdale, c. 1913. (Beamish)

GIRSBY BRIDGE, A BRIDLE BRIDGE OF IRON GIRDERS, was erected in 1870 by Theophania Blackett with Thomas Dyke, civil engineer, in compensation for closing a right of way past Sockburn Hall.

SOCKBURN HALL was rebuilt c. 1834 in a Jacobean style.

THE RUINED CHURCH OF ALL SAINTS', Sockburn, was dismantled when Girsby church opened in 1838. A thirteenth-century church on Saxon foundations, its fifteenth-century Conyers chapel was closed off to preserve sculptured stonework. A grey boulder nearby reputedly has a dragon buried under it, the legendary Sockburn Worm slain by Sir John Conyers.

FISHLOCKS, Dinsdale, c. 1880.

FISHLOCKS WEIR AND MILL on the Tees, c. 1913. Visitors to Dinsdale and Middleton One Row came to see the salmon leap up the fall. There was a productive salmon fishery, and other kinds of fish were plentiful. (Beamish)

SECTION ELEVEN

Neasham

NEASHAM AND THE RIVER TEES. In the row facing the riverside green, Ivy House stands out with its two Wellingtonias dominant in any distant view. Now there is only one. Neasham probably derives its name from the sharp river bend – from Anglo Saxon *naes*, a nose or headland.

MOWING HAY by the Tees. The field belonged to Cresswell Ward of Neasham Hill House and was let out, a pony being pastured on it. The two horses would be hired ones, probably from the Hobsons.

NEASHAM HILL HOUSE, now a retirement home, was built c. 1757 by the Ward family who rebuilt much of the village after the devastating Tees flood of 1771. Ronald and Samuel Ward donated the ornate village pump house and shelter in 1879. The wing on the right was added by Captain Crosby who took these first three photographs.

NEASHAM VILLAGE FROM DINSDALE BANK. Neasham Hill House wall is on the left. Anne Lee remembers pace-eggs and violets in the field on the right. Pace, or paste, (variants of Paschal, the season of Easter) were hard-boiled eggs coloured and decorated, and rolled downhill in competitions at Easter.

A MEET AT NEASHAM opposite the model cottages built by Sir Thomas Wrightson of Neasham Hall in 1902.

THE ROW AT THE EAST END OF NEASHAM. The model cottage adjoined an older row of twelve, of which only two refurbished ones now remain. The sign board indicated the Golden Cock pub which closed in 1958. The long wall enclosed one of the four market garden orchards in Neasham.

THE SAME ROW, looking east, photographed before the Wards built the pump house and shelter at the crossroads in 1879, in which the water spout, now gone, represented the legendary Sockburn Worm. The cart was standing by the Golden Cock.

NEASHAM NATIONAL SCHOOL was built in 1867 as two schoolrooms and a single-storey teacher's cottage, later raised to two storeys, the ground floor then becoming an extra schoolroom. Under Durham County Council from 1927 it became an all-age school, and from 1938 primary only. It closed in 1961 and is now a house. P.T. on the green is remembered.

THE ROW FACING THE GREEN, 1909, included the Hare and Hounds pub, closed in 1955, with its stable and brewhouse behind. At the end was a shop, post office and cobbler's, entered from a gable-end door in a lane leading to a communal yard typical of Neasham rows. Ivy House, built in the 1880s, had gardens, stables and outhouses and was ivy-covered.

THE SAME ROW AND SHOP as on the previous page, looking west to a single elm, now gone, which gave its name to the adjacent Elm Tree Cottage. The green was still rough and had wooden rails.

A TEES FLOOD in front of the same row in the 1960s. The last flood was in 1968, after which a protective embankment was built and the green landscaped.

TEES FLOOD, 1914. The second, higher road on the right was there for use during the regular river floods. In the flood of 1771, all but one house was destroyed. Elm Tree Cottage, ivy-covered, was at one time Warwick's grocery shop and post office. Near it, set into the wall of Orchard House, was Queen Victoria's Jubilee pump house, 1887, later removed.

NEASHAM PEACE CELEBRATIONS, 1919, included a bicycle parade.

THE FOX AND HOUNDS, before its rear and right-hand-side extensions were built. A National Cyclists Union sign is on the wall. On the left was Slipway Lane and a boathouse. In 1651 there was a complaint that the boat maintained by the lord of the manor was missing. The ferry ceased to operate in 1906, but two waths or fords were still negotiable.

AN OLD INN SIGN, SKETCHED BY GEORGE FOTHER-GILL, who commented: 'Mr Forbes, MFH of the Hurworth, hunts the hounds in a top-hat.'

NEASHAM FEAST, photographed here before 1914, was held on the green on the first weekend in August until c. 1926. Dues had to be paid to Cresswell Ward of Neasham Hill House. Former schoolteacher Anne Lee remembers Crow's roundabouts, coconut shies and Granny Noble's yellow and brittle Cinder Toffee.

NEASHAM FEAST, c. 1912. Mr Boulby, on the right, was dressed as a woman. Feast Sunday was the first Sunday in August.

A REAPER AND BINDER of the 1940s behind an early tractor on Neasham Springs Farm, farmed by the Miller family. The binder was bought in 1941, and was 'ground driven'.

WHITE WYANDOTTS, pure bred and free range, outside one of five typical hen huts on Neasham Springs Farm.

NEASHAM BRICKS, 1924. A workers' group in front of the ovens at Neasham Brick Works. The skeleton of an elk, now in Darlington Museum, was found in 1939 in a peat deposit among the glacial clays used for brickmaking. Skip Bridge Works made drainage tiles.

A NATURAL GAS PIPELINE being laid in thick clays across Neasham Springs Farm. The Nymac excavating machine was waterlogged. One machine sank out of sight altogether, and had to be abandoned.

A FOX SHOOT at Neasham Springs Farm.

A STACKYARD SCENE. Raking hay at Neasham Springs Farm.

SECTION TWELVE

Hurworth and Newbus Grange

HURWORTH VILLAGE. The green merges into Church Row, the workaday end where agricultural labourers, craftsmen and the linen weavers, whose Huguenot forebears set up the linen industry here, once lived. Cottages backing on to the Tees were built into solid rock, where damp cellars and garden sheds were the handloom weavers' workshops. The churchyard later lost its iron railings.

NURSE OVENS in the 1920s airing the three young Riley-Lord girls at Newbus Grange. Scylla was the eldest.

THE DRAWING ROOM, Newbus Grange, refurbished after a fire in 1935. The satinwood Steinway piano was blue to match the walls, and ornamented with gold leaf curlicues. Miss Sable, an artist from London, painted scenes of Newbus Grange gardens on the panels.

NEWBUS GRANGE was built in 1610, but much altered in the nineteenth century, when it received a castellated Regency Gothic treatment with perpendicular tracery, a cast-iron first-floor verandah and interior panelling. Between the wars, and until c. 1962, the Riley-Lords lived there, adding the large bay. Now it is a hotel.

E. SCYLLA RILEY-LORD and one of her sisters in the garden.

CARTING HAY in Newbus Grange meadow before the Second World War.

THE FROZEN TEES near Newbus Grange, looking towards Neasham, also before the Second World War.

THE TEMPERANCE HALL AND READING ROOM, Hurworth, accommodated 250. It was designed in 1864 by architect G.G. Hoskins, then living in Hurworth as clerk of the works to Alfred Waterhouse who was building Pilmore mansion for the Quaker banker Alfred Backhouse. Now the village hall, it has lost its iron railings but gained a porch.

THE BAY HORSE, HURWORTH, a coaching inn believed to be originally fifteenth-century in date. It faces the churchyard where, some say, wives hid behind tombstones to berate their husbands on leaving the pub. The sundial over the coach arch is dated 1739. The one-storey building on the corner of Coach Lane was a smithy.

THE TAPERING GREEN, C. 1900. The trees on the left mark Hurworth Manor garden. The houses on the left were probably Georgian, with Victorian bays added.

HURWORTH MOOR HOUSE, designed by Clark and Moscrop of Darlington in 1890 for the wedding of Edward Lloyd Pease with Helen Pease, and completed in 1891 by MacKenzie, also of Darlington.

HURWORTH MANOR. The manor with an early eighteenth-century façade and 'HBE 1728' marked on the downspouts was later owned by William Batty Wrightson. Early in the present century Reginald Pease, younger brother of Edward Lloyd Pease of Hurworth Moor House, lived here. Both were sons of Henry Pease of Pierremont.

KITCHEN MAIDS in the garden of Hurworth Manor, c. 1900.

THE HURWORTH HERMIT. Old Jack Tiplady (Jacky Tip) lived and died at Church Row next to the river. In the 1840s and '50s four members of the Tiplady family were linen weavers in Hurworth.

CROFT SPA STATION, HURWORTH PLACE, looking south towards the Hurworth road bridge which was raised in height as early as c. 1960 in anticipation of main line electrification. The gas lamps are a reminder of the Croft and Hurworth Gasworks and a coal depot built alongside the original Croft Branch of the Stockton and Darlington Railway nearer the Tees.

CROFT SPA STATION, looking north. The Croft Branch of the S & DR, 1829, was left as a siding when this line was opened in 1841 as the Great North of England Railway from York to Darlington. This station also served the later Richmond line. It closed, probably when the Richmond line was abandoned during the Beeching closures. Visitors to the spa lodged on both sides of the Tees.

THE COMET HOTEL, HURWORTH PLACE, named after the famous Shorthorn bull 'Comet', sold in 1910 by Charles Colling of Ketton Hall. Charles then retired to Monk End Hall, Croft.

CROFT BRIDGE, 6 March 1963, in flood after a sudden thaw ended a three-month freeze-up. Ice floes bump the piers in the picture. On Croft Bridge, new bishops first entering their Durham diocese are presented with the falchion with which Sir John Conyers reputedly slew the Sockburn Worm. Bishop Jenkins continued the tradition. The ancient bridge was restored in 1673 and widened. Tolls were abolished in 1879.

HELL KETTLES, 1964, ponds famed to travellers. A twelfth-century chronicler described a cataclysmic origin for this feature on Christmas Day 1179. It was later believed to be an earthquake or gaseous explosion. Legends abounded – bottomless pits, a monstrous pike, a farmer, horse and cart lost without trace. This is now a site of special scientific interest.

Blackwell and the River Tees

BLACKWELL SCHOOL AND THE ANGEL INN at Bland's Corner. The inn served the Coal Road (Carmel Road), the Great North Road and the Bridge Road. Converted by Eliza Barclay in 1873 into a training school for servants, it became a British School where Quakers and Methodists held services on alternate Sundays, then an elementary school, the teacher of which, Mrs Boswell, is still remembered. Bland's garage took its place.

BLACKWELL HILL LODGE BESIDE BRIDGE ROAD, the 'Angel Inn to Barton Lane End Turnpike Road', which crossed the Tees via the newly built Blackwell Bridge of 1832. This narrow road became the A1. The lodge with a datestone 1869 was designed by G.G. Hoskins.

WIDENING BLACKWELL BRIDGE, February 1960. The narrow bridge of Gatherley Moor sandstone designed by John and Benjamin Green of Newcastle replaced a ford and ferry over the Tees. The toll-house, centre right, on the Yorkshire end is still there.

BLACKWELL HILL, perched above the Tees near Blackwell bridge, was designed c. 1870 by G.G. Hoskins for Eliza Barclay, widow of Robert Barclay and sister of John Church Backhouse. Later the home of Edward and Rachael Backhouse Mounsey, it passed to G.M. Harroway, founding benefactor of Elm Ridge Methodist Church, and then to John Neasham. It was demolished c. 1970 to build the houses of Farr Holme.

BROKEN SCAR DAM UNDER CONSTRUCTION in 1930. A view across the Tees to the Durham bank and houses along Coniscliffe Road.

HILL CLOSE HOUSE FARM formerly belonged to the Allan family of Blackwell. This barn and stable along Nunnery Lane has now been converted into a house.

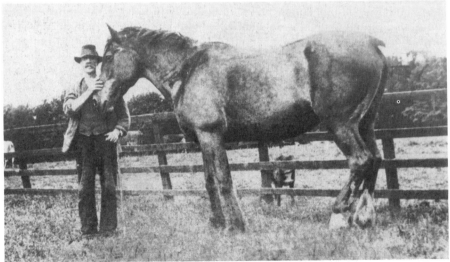

TED FORSTER WITH A CARTHORSE, C. 1910, in the paddock below Hill Close House Farm. Previously a lead-miner, he had farmed at The Ashes, Mickleton and at Springfield. Here, he broke horses in, kept cows and fished for salmon in the Tees. He died in 1915. During the First World War soldiers camped in this paddock, and officers lodged in the farmhouse.

FREDERICK LOVERSIDGE OF DARLINGTON, by the Tees near Blackwell Bridge, c. 1900, with four salmon all weighing over 20 lb. He was also known for his prize-winning fox terriers, great danes and rabbits, and was awarded the Imperial Service Medal for his work with Darlington Post Office.

GEORGE KIRKUP, well-known fly fisherman in the Tees near Broken Scar, 1932. Darlington waterworks chimney is behind.

THREE ANGLERS in 1931, who worked together in Darlington as signwriters for seventeen years: Carl Birkbeck, Arthur Dixon and Albert Bell.

FREDERICK CARL BIRKBECK, May 1931, a well-known member of Darlington Anglers' Club from 1930 and now its longest surviving member. On Easter Monday 1936 he caught above Blackwell Bridge on his own fly, Snipe and Purple, a sea trout 22 in long.

BROWN TROUT CAUGHT ON FLY in 1943 at Blackwell by Carl Birkbeck. At that time the lower size limit was 9 in. Now, when fish are scarcer, it is 11 in, and numbers are limited.

THE FROZEN TEES ABOVE BROKEN SCAR DAM, 22 December 1962. This was the beginning of an exceptionally long, cold winter when rivers and waterfalls froze over for three months, ending in a sudden overnight thaw on 5/6 March 1963 with spectacular results.

THE TEES IN FURY BELOW BROKEN SCAR DAM, 6 March 1963. Ice floes knock the bank on the left.

Darlington Countrygoers

DARLINGTON AND TEESDALE NATURALISTS' FIELD CLUB MEMBERS wield geological hammers for rock or fossil specimens on a visit to a quarry. A lady botanist has picked flowers. Collecting specimens is no longer acceptable. Observation, recording and photography are now the rule. The club will celebrate its centenary in 1991.

DARLINGTON FIELD CLUB OUTING, 1913. Men, from the left: James Broadhead, Mr Crow, H.E. Temple, William Mossom, J. Buckle, Mr Bishop and Mr O'Wheeler. Three centre ladies: Mrs Gregory, Mrs Temple and Miss Hammond.

POND DIPPING AT HELL KETTLES, 1964, with the permission of Mr John Fell, Oxen-le-Fields Farm. Darlington Field Club members from the left: Ray Ritchie, Hilda Worthington, Vic Brown, Dorothy Jenkinson, Ada Radford, -?-, -?-

THE 8TH DARLINGTON (COCKERTON) CUBS and others, in 1918, beside the Tees at Blackwell. Scouts in the background: E. Watts, Fred Hughes, Mrs Brigham, Percy Brigham, Danny Pawson, Mr J. Baker, ? Wheeler and Tom Curtiss.

DARLINGTON 13TH SCOUT TROOP and trek cart ready for Annual Camp, in 1944. Wartime shortages affected uniforms. From the left: Edwin Turnbull, Colin Barker, William Henderson, William Wilson (scoutmaster), Frank Beadle, Douglas Saunders and Jack Dent. Destination: Borrowdale.

JOHN MADDISON, SCOUTMASTER, showing one of the books presented to five Queen's Scouts in 1958 at Dodmire School at the Annual Parents' Meeting of the 13th Darlington Scouts' Group.

DARLINGTON CYCLE CLUB, established in 1876, was one of the first cyclists' clubs in the country. Sir Joseph Whitwell Pease was the first president. Members wore a uniform of velvet jacket and drab cord light breeches. Two years later, a green fine cloth jacket and velvet cord trousers were worn. In 1883 they changed to a cavalry uniform.

DARLINGTON CYCLE CLUB MEMBERS pause on a ride in the 1940s. Plus fours, knee breeches or long socks kept trouser legs out of oily bicycle chains. The club was disbanded c. 1970.

BOYS' BRIGADE CAMP at Neasham Springs Farm, before the Second World War.

DARLINGTON HOLIDAY FELLOWSHIP and Cooperative Holidays Association Ramblers crossing Girsby Bridge to Sockburn in 1934. On the left, the leader, Reg Butler, a pre-war H.F. Official. In front, Kathy Blackburn; Margaret Holliday behind.

A HORSE AND TRAP OUTSIDE THE BUCK INN on Sadberge green. The age of the horse in travel, transport and farming virtually ended with the Second World War. Horses and smithies rapidly disappeared.

ACKNOWLEDGEMENTS

This volume is based mainly on the private collections of local people together with photographs I took during the rapid changes of the 1960s. In every case I have taken care to establish ownership and copyright. If any errors have occurred, I do apologise.

My grateful thanks go to those who so kindly allowed me to copy their photographs:
Beatrice Alsop • Mike Anderson • Dorothy Arthur • Pat Barnaby
Sheila Barnett • Eric Bell • Carl Birkbeck • Marjorie Brown • Richard Brown
Dot Burton • Stan Cardwell • Fiona Carr • T.J. Chapman • James Clarke
D.A. Danby • Darlington and Teesdale Naturalists' Field Club • 8th Darlington
(BP) Scout Group • 13th Darlington Scout Group • Annie M. Dennis
Dinsdale Spa Golf Club • J. Elliott • J.W. Fell • Alan Fraser • Beatrice Futter
Phyllis Garrod • Anne Graham • J.H. Gunn • R.W. Hewitson • Flossie Hill
Richard Holland • Bill Lawson • Anne Lee • Ian Leonard • Pamela Longstaffe
I.R. MacKenzie • John Maddison • Norman Miller • George Nixon
Theresa Reay • Roma Reed • Audrey Reid • P.B. Reynolds • Edna Richardson
Scylla Riley-Lord • George Scott • Gordon Sims • Joan Tinkler • Annie Usher
Jennifer Wain • Edward Ward • Betty Walters • Doris Whatmore
Mary Woodthorpe

Those who helped me to find or interpret photographs include:
Joy Atkinson •T.R. Bell • E.M. Blakeway • Brendan Boyle • Betty Cooper
Jill Goldson • Andrew Guy • Pauline Haslam • Tom Hay • Phyllis Hornsey
Hilary W. Jackson • Patty Lumb • Joyce MacKenzie • Mary Mitchinson
Basil Noble • Margaret Port • Betty Richardson • Natalie E. Urquhart
Dot Weaver • A.W. Wilson and P.J. Wright

Beamish North of England Open Air Museum, Darlington District Library, Darlington Museum and the *Northern Echo* have also allowed me to include photographs from their collections.

Alan Suddes encouraged me to undertake this volume.